SCOTLAND
A MODERN MISCELLANY

JUMPED UP PUBLISHING
EDINBURGH

SCOTLAND
A MODERN MISCELLANY

MICHAEL KERRIGAN & RONNIE SCOTT
with ART BY ADAM LARKUM, INK-TANK & ASSOCIATES

1 Skara Brae
2 Helmsdale
3 Culloden
4 Glencoe
5 Aberlemno
6 Kilmartin Glen
7 Loch Lomond & the
    Trossachs Nat. Park
8 Bannockburn
9 Largs
10 Whithorn

Shetland,
Fair Isle

Orkney

1

John o'Groats

Durness   Thurso

2

Lewis   Ullapool

St
Kilda

Moray Firth

Elgin

Inverness

3

Cairngorms
National Park

Aberdeen

North
Uist   Skye

Aviemore

Fort
Augustus

Stonehaven

Fort William

4

Pitlochry

Brechin

Oban

6

5

Arbroath

Jura

Perth   Dundee

7

St Andrews

Arran   Stirling

8

Mull of
Kintyre   Firth of
                 Clyde   Glasgow   Falkirk   Firth of Forth

9   Edinburgh

Ayr   New Lanark

Berwick-
upon-
Tweed

Melrose

Stranraer

Dumfries

Kirkcudbright   Gretna

10

CONTENTS

'Here's tae us. Wha's like us?' asked Robert Burns, our national bard, in one of his famous toasts. 'No one' is the answer. For such a wee country, Scotland has many sides. Its long, action-packed history means you're never far from a castle, a museum or a Neolithic standing stone. Meanwhile, the dramatic Highlands and the equally spectacular Lowlands and our woodlands, lochs and coasts make this an unrivalled destination in scenic terms. And don't forget your binoculars, because there's an abundance of timorous beasties in the mountains, glens and rivers, from red squirrels and otters to red deer and ospreys.

Then there's the culture and traditions. Don your finest tartan and check out one of our award-winning whisky distilleries or our increasingly popular real ales; or why not visit Rabbie Burns' birthplace and learn more about the people and places that inspired him? All of these braw bits of Scotland add up to one of the most vibrant countries in the world. This book brings all of these sides together, introducing you to the miscellany that makes up Caledonia.

Scotland is abuzz with beautiful flora and fauna in every type of landscape, including rugged mountains, fertile machairs, unspoilt golden beaches and silver lochs. There's so much to see and marvel at, and you'll find inspiration in these pages that will tempt you to discover more of our natural heritage for yourself.

People have been making this land their home since the Stone Age, and you can see remnants of the past everywhere: from ancient stone circles and burial chambers to Pictish monuments, from the ruined cathedral at St Andrews to Stirling Castle and Bannockburn. There are also museums and entire towns that celebrate our industry and commerce, which has bounced back from the decline of heavy engineering and fully embraced the new digital economy.

All of these historical sites can be found in our exciting cities, tranquil towns and glorious countryside, and this wee book gives you a guided tour of the best bits. Head up to the Great Glen where the Loch Ness Monster awaits you. Keep driving and you'll be in the heart of the Highlands – or take the scenic train route over the Glenfinnan Viaduct – and the dramatic landscapes of the Islands are no more than a ferry ride away.

You'll always be given a warm welcome in our largest city, Glasgow, with its eclectic array of architecture and host of friendly, buzzing music venues, bars and galleries. The capital, Edinburgh, has its own unique mix of old and new: its looming castle and winding alleyways rub up against restaurants, bookshops and kilt-makers, the International Festival and the brand-new tramway. Finish off your trip in the diverse scenery of the Borders, or with a spot of golf on the 'Royal and Ancient' course at St Andrews.

Last, but by no means least, is Scotland's inimitable culture. Not only does our literary canon boast such greats as Robert Burns, we're also at the forefront of scientific innovations, as the birthplace of Dolly the Sheep and medical ultrasound. Kilts and bagpipes are strong symbols of the country's past and present – you can still hear the hum of the pipes in our cities and see young men wearing their tartan kilts with pride. And let's not forget the food! Scottish cuisine is packed with delicious delights ranging from the savoury to the extra sweet: pick up a tin of buttery shortbread, or join a Burns Night supper and dig into a plateful of haggis, neeps and tatties.

Whether its culture, scenery or culinary delicacies you're after, you'll never go hungry in Scotland. This modern mix of Scottish nature, history, places and traditions captures the heart of our small but mighty nation. Welcome to the biggest wee country in the world!

BONNIE BANKS,
BRAES & BEASTIES

Scotland is famous throughout the world for its virtually unrivalled natural beauty: little wonder, then, that the celebrated 'Land of the Mountain and the Flood' is the destination of choice for anyone seeking spectacular scenery.

This chapter provides a brief introduction to the wonderful variety of landscapes, habitats and wildlife in this small gem of a country. Striking geological features such as sheer cliffs and deep lochs and faultlines provide drama aplenty, as do crashing waves and roaring waterfalls. Peace and solitude may be found in the primeval pinewoods and quiet birch groves. Those in search of wide vistas may head for the open moors and marshlands, or for rugged mountains in the Grampians and Northwest Highlands, or perhaps along the shores of some of our unspoilt silver lochs.

A home to golden eagles, ospreys, gannets, grouse, otters, deer, red squirrels, dolphins and salmon, and all sorts of other birds, mammals, plants and marine life, Scotland has more wildlife to the square metre than any other part of the UK. Thistles may be the most famous national wildflower, but heather and orchids, bluebells and irises abound too. And biodiversity is being boosted by the addition of reintroduced species, notably beavers and white-tailed sea eagles, which help to restore nature's order in their respective habitats.

Whether your preference is for national parks and visitor centres where you can study the rocks, farm animals, sealife and ecosystems, or for action-packed outdoor sports, or the wilderness experience so that you can simply escape in a glorious setting, Scotland has an abundance of natural treasures.

All that remains is to wish you joyous times exploring Scotland's 'bonnie banks and braes' (from Burns' poem 'Ye Banks and Braes o' Bonnie Doon'). Don't forget to bring your waterproofs!

Water, Water, Everywhere

A land of 'torrents and loud-pouring floods,' wrote Burns. He knew what he was talking about – that's for sure. Marked as it is with deep, jagged inlets, the country's coastline is out of all proportion to its size: the mainland's coast alone measures 6,718km (4,174 miles); add in the islands and it's more than twice that long. And there isn't too much dry ground in between, what with 560-odd lochs, covering over 880 square km (340 square miles) – not to mention marshes, morasses, bogs, rivers and streams. That's a *lot* of water, and we haven't even mentioned the rain (yet).

Sailing, windsurfing, kayaking, canoeing, fishing, diving, rafting, wakeboarding: we've got all the watersports!

Rain

All those lochs and rivers don't come from nowhere, and neither does the luxuriant green: Scotland's climate is consistently damp and dreich, especially in the western Highlands, where it rains and rains. The average annual rainfall here is just over 4.58m (180 inches). Not that it's monotonous, you understand: apart from the occasional torrent, there are sudden downpours, persistent rain, brief showers, light drizzle and the peculiarly penetrating precipitation that rejoices in the title of 'Scotch Mist'. If the sun is blazing, don't worry: it'll likely rain again soon – except perhaps on Tiree, the island that claims to be the sunniest place in the UK.

There's no such thing as bad weather, only the wrong clothes, according to Billy Connolly.

Famous Firths

A firth is an overgrown inlet of the sea;
a wide river estuary, fjord or sea loch:
the map of Scotland's coastline is clearly
punctuated by these jagged cleavages.
Edinburgh stands on one, the Firth of
Forth; Dundee to the north lies on the
Firth of Tay: these two indentations
mark out Fife as a separate 'kingdom'.
On the opposite coast, the Firth of Clyde
is the dominant feature of southwestern
Scotland – almost a sea in itself, with the
Isle of Arran at its centre. And there's the
Solway Firth, the Firth of Pentland, Lorn,
Dornoch, Cromarty, Moray, Beauly and
several more in the Northern Isles…

*The inner Firth of Clyde has long carried cargo vessels
as well as passengers cruising 'doon the watter'.*

Cliffs

Scotland's coastline is one of its glories, with its golden beaches, rolling dunes and marshes: sometimes, though, the country ends much more abruptly. Some of the most spectacular cliffs in the world are to be seen here: from St Abb's Head, north of Berwick, all the way round to the Mull of Galloway, and not forgetting the islands – especially the Outer Hebrides and Orkney.

A scenic marvel, they're also a great natural resource, and a home to seabird colonies and rare plants and insect species. But the dramatic, jagged coastline is hazardous, too. Pioneering engineer Robert Stevenson (Robert Louis' grandfather) worked wonders to safeguard seafarers with his world-renowned lighthouses.

A bracing clifftop walk along the Berwickshire coast will take you to the heights of North Sea birdwatching.

The Northern Isles

The archipelagos of Orkney and Shetland are rugged, wind-whipped, wave-lashed landscapes where geological features such as sea stacks and arches plainly reveal the mighty power of these forces of erosion. The islands even have their own animal subspecies, like the Orkney vole and the Shetland wren. Further from the mainland, Shetland is more removed in other ways too, with its indigenous sheepdogs, geese and, most famously, diminutive ponies. But perhaps the most striking feature of these islands is actually an absence – the winds here are so strong that there are virtually no trees at all.

Rising 137m (449 ft) from the sea, the Old Man of Hoy, off Orkney, is Britain's highest sea stack.

Beaches and Bays

Some of Scotland's finest beaches are also among its most remote: the Northwest Highlands and Western Isles are particularly blessed with fine, white sands lapped by aquamarine waters – Luskentyre Beach on Harris, for example. The eastern end of the John Muir Way connects a series of beaches just a pebble's throw from Edinburgh; visitors to the East Neuk of Fife are spoilt for choice; while Ayrshire and Dumfries and Galloway also boast miles of sandy shores for a bracing walk or swim. And though you're never far from the coast in Scotland, there are inland beaches, too: Luss Beach is one of many along Loch Lomond's banks.

Jura's west coast boasts several examples of 'raised beaches' – formed as a result of sea-level changes during the Ice Age.

The Quiraing

Standing atop the Quiraing and looking out across the sea or south over the Isle of Skye is a profoundly moving experience – quite literally. For this rugged mountainside – the eastern slope of Meall na Suiramach – is inching slowly but steadily downhill, making it the largest active landslip in Great Britain. The scenery isn't just beautiful but joltingly dramatic, otherworldly even. From the sudden spike of the Needle, 37m (120ft) high, to the equally unexpected flatness of the Table, this is a landscape to astonish and amaze. Little wonder, then, that it appears in movies from Ridley Scott's *Prometheus* to the latest interpretation of *Macbeth*.

Despite its defining features being its jagged spikes, the Norse for 'round fold' gave the Quiraing its name.

The Great Glen

The Northwest Highlands and the rest of Scotland were originally separate landmasses, formed far apart on different geological 'plates'. About 400 million years ago, they were brought together by 'continental drift'. This epic collision produced a faultline that runs all the way from Loch Linnhe to the Moray Firth – a stretch of 100km (62 miles). Mountains were forced up on either side by the impact, but the fault itself formed a gigantic fissure – hence the depth of Loch Ness, which lies in the northern section of the Great Glen. The Highland Boundary Fault is the second distinctive faultline across Scotland, running from Arran to Stonehaven, via Comrie, Perthshire, where Earthquake House measures seismic activity.

One long rift dividing the nation –
in purely geological terms, of course!

Munros & Corbetts

In 1891 Sir Hugh Munro drew up his table of Scotland's highest mountains, identifying all those summits – 'Munros' – over 3,000ft (914m) above sea level. Since then, enthusiastic hillwalkers have engaged in 'Munro bagging' – climbing as many of the Munros as possible. It's a task made all the more difficult by the fact that the list of 'Munros' regularly changes. Classification gets fantastically technical as, below its peak or summit, a mountain may have multiple lower 'tops'. For those that fail to make the Munro grade (or lose that status), all is not lost: John Rooke Corbett drew up his list of peaks above 2,500ft (762m) in the 1920s.

So many peaks (283 Munros and 449 Corbetts at the last count)… yet so little time…

Arthur's Seat

There should, you'd think, be a legend attached to this mountain-ette which manages to dominate Edinburgh so dramatically, despite being no more than 251m (823ft) high. There's no suggestion that King Arthur ever sat here, though, beyond the name. What *did* sit here, over 300 million years ago, was a volcano – now thankfully extinct. It was all worn away by glaciers during the Ice Age, apart from the hard basalt plug. There's quite a sprinkling of these volcanic plugs in the city of Edinburgh and its environs: Castle Rock's another, as are North Berwick Law and the Bass Rock.

From one volcanic plug to another: Arthur's Seat and the Castle are twin peaks on the Edinburgh skyline.

Red Squirrel

Scotland is home to more than four-fifths of the UK's surviving red squirrel population. The russet rodent – which boasts the nation's indigenous hair colour – has been the victim of persistent bullying since its bigger, greyer relatives arrived from across the Pond.

Sharing the red squirrel's fondness for tree-climbing in the Caledonian Forest habitat is the sleek and nimble pine marten. Around the size of a cat, the pine marten faced near-extinction a century ago, but its population has rebounded. Maybe it could teach squirrels a thing or two about survival.

Squirrels spend their autumn days stocking up food caches for the chill days of winter.

Red Deer

A symbol of Scottish prestige,
proud and majestic, the red deer stag
appears on postcards and souvenirs and is
a favourite photo subject. Its success as a
species is double-edged, however. With
no natural predator, overgrown herds
roam large areas of the Highlands, often
breaching fences designed to contain
them. They're a menace to the trees
they strip of bark and the saplings they
graze – and a threat to their fellow roe
and fallow deer, as available grazing is
exhausted. So has the stag fallen from its
pedestal to be grouped alongside rats as a
'pest'? O, the ignominy!

*Deer are not just for Christmas (cards): venison is
a highly prized food, for both taste and nutrition.*

Comeback Creatures

Over the centuries, many of Scotland's native species have disappeared from the countryside, perhaps because of excessive hunting, or habitat loss. Reintroducing these animals – such as beavers, which became extinct 400 years ago – helps reinvigorate biodiversity. That's certainly how conservationists see it, but the idea of bringing back predators like the wolf (the last one was killed in 1769) is controversial, with some farmers and landowners vehemently opposed to reintroducing species that might kill livestock or damage landscapes. But reintroductions can benefit people also: the sea eagle has been a great boon to tourism on the Islands.

Our recently reintroduced beavers made themselves at home first in the Knapdale Forest in Argyll.

Otter

What we know as the 'European otter' can be found from Scandinavia to Sumatra. But Scotland is where it's at for the UK otter. Over half of the total population is here, with a big proportion of those living in the Highlands and Islands. Even if they weren't, though, the otter would still be inseparably associated with north-west Scotland on account of Gavin Maxwell's famous book, *Ring of Bright Water*. You'll be doing well to see one, however, widespread though they are. Otters are by no means introverted: they're lively and engaging among friends, but they come over all shy and elusive when we're around.

Otters are well adapted for fishing: they have webbed feet and can close their ears and nostrils whilst underwater.

Highland Coo

They've been farmed for many centuries now, and temperamentally they tend towards gentleness, but Highland cattle still have an alarmingly undomesticated air. Those long, spreading horns look lethal, though they're very seldom deployed in anger; then there's that dense, shaggy coat of russet fur. It's the latter that enables the animal to brave blizzards, icy cold, driving rain, hail, fog and all the other delights of the Scottish climate. Add to this their ability to survive on the sparsest, scabbiest grass, and they're fully equipped to face the rigours of the Highland scene.

The mighty hielan coo: bulls can weigh anything up to 800kg (1,800lbs).

Galloway Beltie

Short and stocky, and mostly black,
the Belted Galloway gets its name
from the broad white stripe around its
middle, which sets its apart from all the
other Scottish cows (it's also known as
the Oreo cow, for its resemblance to
the American cookie). It's been on the
scene – largely, as its name suggests,
in the southwest of the country – for
centuries. The Beltie, bred for its beef,
is much less widely known than the
Aberdeen Angus, but most experts
consider that its beautifully marbled
meat leaves all competition far behind,
even that of its northerly neighbour.

Their high-visibility belt is a boon to herders in dim light:
Highland drovers liked to include a Beltie in their stock.

Sheep

No drive through the Highlands would be quite complete without a half-hour hold-up while a flock of sheep is moved from field to field, or simply wanders on to the road of its own accord. The hardy Scottish Blackface is the most familiar sheep (not just in Scotland but in Britain as a whole), and their wool is used in the production of Harris Tweed. A great variety of other breeds are to be found as well, though, from the Soay – which is thought to date back to Neolithic times, and descended from the feral sheep of St Kilda – to the North Ronaldsay, which lives largely on seaweed.

Wool from the mountain-grazing Blackface sheep is used in carpets and mattresses as well as tweeds.

Giant Panda

The red squirrel may be charming; the red deer may be majestic; but for sheer charisma what could possibly beat a panda? Big and slow and fantastically furry, with doleful black eye-patches on a cute round face: what other animal can look cool simply by sitting there chewing bamboo? Panda-mania gripped Scotland when Sichuan sensation Tian Tian ('Sweetie') arrived at Edinburgh Zoo with her mate Yang Guang, or 'Sunshine'. At least, he is supposed to be her mate: for the most part they've been going their separate ways so far, though; that panda cuddliness only seems to go fur-deep.

These representatives of the rarest members of the bear family are Scotland's most popular visitors. Ever!

Gannet

This oft-maligned seabird is the largest
in Europe, and the most easily spotted
because of its contrasting plumage. But
this is Scotland, so, whether in football,
confectionery, architecture, or the 'quality
of the light', you'll find east- and west-coast
rivalries. Depending where you hail from,
then, your 'favourite' gannet colony will be
East Lothian's Bass Rock, or Ailsa Craig in
the Firth of Clyde. Soaring above the sea
on long, straight wings, the gannet plunges
down spectacularly when it spots a fish. The
dazzling-white appearance of its nesting sites
confirms that, famous as it is for gluttony, all
this eating makes it a productive bird too.

*Gannets dive at speeds of up to 100kmh (62mph)
as they hit the water in search of fish.*

Osprey

This black-and-white (or brown-and-white) fish-eating hawk, which has a call like a whistle, was to be found around lakes across Britain before being wiped out in the 19th century. There was huge excitement when, in 1954, a pair of Scandinavian exiles set up home at Loch Garten. Disappointingly, though, they didn't breed (reminding us of those other creatures with black eye-patches, now in residence at the zoo). Fortunately, ospreys have made up for lost time in the decades since: today there are hundreds across Scotland – and beyond – sojourning here in the light summer months.

There are few sights as magnificent as an osprey, wings outstretched, seizing its prey.

Red Grouse

Famous from the label of the whisky bottle, the grouse doesn't actually partake – though the flushed-red wattle above its eye might lead one to imagine otherwise. On the contrary, it has the healthiest of diets: what else would it be in an environment running with spring water (£1.50 a bottle to you and me) and packed with soft green heather-shoots and blaeberries (the latest superfood)? Any chance of a sedentary lifestyle is put paid to by the annual explosion of gunfire that comes with the 'Glorious 12th' of August, which marks the start of the hunting season.

Red grouse and heather go together like…
well… like birds of a feather.

Salmon

The salmon is the leaping Lord of the Highland River, though up-close it has a less than regal appearance, with its goggly staring eye. It helps to be a monarch (or a millionaire) yourself if you want to try your hand at salmon fishing: a prestigious pitch can set you back several hundred pounds a day. At the same time, all the salmon farms that have sprung up on the west coast means that this most aristocratic of fish is now practically the people's food. A wild salmon will spend up to four years at sea, migrating as far as Greenland: perhaps the distance swimming is the secret to its matchless, delicate flavour.

Returning salmon must leap 3.7m (12ft) to clear the Orrin Falls in Ross-shire.

Marine Treasures

The best-kept secret of Scotland's deeps is arguably not the Loch Ness Monster, but the cold-water coral reefs in the Atlantic off our shores. Scenes of life and colour down here would give the Great Barrier Reef a run for its money – but most Scots are completely unaware of them. Just as we're not all *au fait* with Scottish seafood in all its incredible variety of tastes and textures. From scallops and squid to monkfish and mussels; from crabs and lobsters to sardines and prawns. Much of this abundance ends up in the tapas bars of Spain, but many of us are partial to our seafood here at home, too.

Oban calls itself the 'Seafood Capital of Scotland', and a number of fishing ports could make similar claims.

Dolphin

Scotland's seas are home to an incredible variety of marine life: inevitably, though, it's the mammals that often seem to excite us most. Intelligent, exuberant and overflowing with what it's hard to resist calling 'personality', the bottlenose dolphin is especially appealing. Crowds turn out to watch these creatures cavorting in the Moray Firth from the shore at Chanonry Point and at the Dolphin Centres at Spey Bay and North Kessock. The latter is good for seeing seals as well, including the (paradoxically rare) common seal as well as the generally much more widespread grey.

Dolphins are present in the Moray Firth year-round, but are easier to spot in summer when they're feeding on salmon.

Midgie

Culicoides impunctatus: behind that Latin name lurks a frightening predator; why reintroduce the wolf when we have something just as alarming in insect form? A miniature mosquito, the midge makes up for its diminutive stature with the ferocity of its attack during the long summer twilights of the Highlands and Islands. The female of the species is definitely more deadly than the male: she's the one who wears the troosers when it comes to biting. Sucking blood as nourishment for her eggs, she leaves a legacy of intense irritation and frantic scratching. Midgie misery…

If it's rainy, cheer up, the midges will stay away.
And if it's midgie heaven, cheer up, it's not raining.

Heather

Calluna vulgaris or 'common heather' it's called, but this really is a flower of rare beauty. It makes a good symbol for Scotland too – and not just because it's so widespread across the wilds of the Highlands. There's something about those delicately beautiful little bells of purple petals strung from a wiry stalk (so tough that it can be made into brooms) that sums up this country in all its contradictions. Heather has traditionally been used for a multitude of purposes: bedding, thatching, rope-making and weaving. The flowers can be used to make dye, or even a delicious tea. Long live our 'fragrant hills of purple heather' in all their matchless glory!

Heather is a gorgeous sight, but useful too – not least for its bee-product, heather honey.

Thistle

The thistle is the perfect flower to represent
Scotland. It's just like us in defensive mode:
spiky, hardy. When Norse invaders crept
ashore for a surprise attack at Largs in 1263,
a barefoot warrior trod on a thistle and
cried out, saving the day for Scotland. The
fearsome flower became a national emblem,
commemorated on James III's silver coins,
the *Encyclopedia Britannica*, in heraldry, poetry
and football club names. Tough and resilient,
the thistle takes unkindly to being chewed by
bovine oppressors. What's not to like? Indeed,
not only is our bonnie bloom found growing
wild everywhere from coast to city verge, it's
become a favourite for fancy florists too.

'Thistle do nicely!'
The flower that fights back.

Caledonian Forest

Scotland isn't short of a tree or two: after the great conifer epidemic of the 1950s and '60s came the tax-deductible timber stands of the '70s. But native woodland was becoming thin on the ground. To some extent, our rocky and mountainous terrain is tough going for trees. Even so, a forest of Scots pine once extended across much of the nation, not to mention mixed woodlands of birch, oak, ash, hazel, alder and willow. Only remnants of the Caledonian Forest still exist today, but regeneration is well under way and our woodlands are among the nation's glories again, with very special ecosystems of their own.

Remnants of the Caledonian Forest support wildlife, including the endangered capercaillie.

Birch Woods

Scotland may not be the only country
with silver birches to boast of, but they're
certainly a special feature of the Scottish
scene. Slender, supple and exquisite,
from its flaky tinfoil bark to its fine
light-green leaves, it's an adornment
to many an otherwise barren brae.
Quintessentially Scottish in being at its
best when it's up against it, birch looks
even better, perhaps, in the long, bleak
months of winter. Look up and see the
tracery of bare twigs against a clear blue
January sky and you have the impression
of a shimmering purplish aura. And that's
only one of our native birches!

*The Gaelic name for silver birch is 'beith' – hence the
Ayrshire town, and placenames like Cowdenbeath, in Fife.*

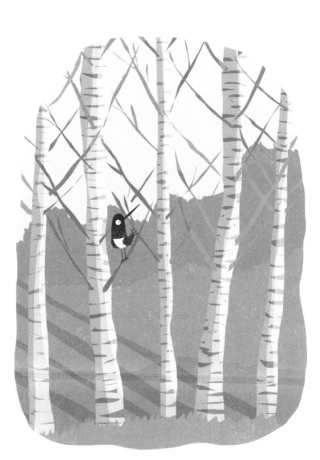

FOR AULD
LANG SYNE

For a wee country, as people from much larger nations often observe, Scotland has an awful lot of history. And, as Burns himself says in his most famous song, we should celebrate 'auld lang syne' (which roughly translates as 'the good old days').

This chapter, like Scotland itself, is packed with history. Of course it's impossible to include everything that's happened in the last few millennia, but you'll find here the essential facts you need to understand this country, to make sense of the places and the people, and bring the past to life. Along the way we've included the most exciting events and fascinating stories, just for good measure.

The story of Scotland is one of conflict and change, of invasions and inventions, and all of these have left their marks on the landscape, on the towns and cities and the Scottish identity. This land is cluttered with evidence of a long and illustrious history: from the prehistoric settlements and monuments of Orkney, Shetland and the Outer Hebrides to the grand houses, city halls and galleries that are the legacy of the great wealth earned in the Industrial Revolution.

Naturally it's not all been plain sailing, with Romans and Vikings, the Wars of Independence and Religion, and the Jacobite Risings. The highs have been very high: think of the great philosophers, economists, architects and scientists that emerged during the Enlightenment. But the lows have been pretty low: the terrible human cost of the Highland Clearances and the witch-hunts of the 17th century.

However, it's this rollercoaster of ups and downs that makes Scottish history so fascinating and complex. We hope you'll enjoy discovering more about this land of Celts and Picts, of kings and queens, of soldiers and saints.

Prehistoric Scotland

People have flocked to Scotland for thousands of years, and Skara Brae on Orkney is one of the first places they put down roots. A community of Stone Age farmers, fishermen and hunters lived in this linked group of houses 5,000 years ago. The stone circles at Callanish on Lewis show that our Bronze Age ancestors understood astronomy and geometry 4,000 years ago. Eildon Hill Fort in the Borders was first occupied 3,000 years ago, and other early Scots lived on crannogs (houses on stilts in the middle of lochs), safe from wolves and other enemies. You can see reconstructed crannogs at the Scottish Crannog Centre in Loch Tay.

The Neolithic settlement at Skara Brae is at least as old as the Pyramids of Egypt.

The Romans in Scotland

The Romans made several incursions into Scotland, but could not maintain a presence north of Hadrian's Wall, which they built around AD 125 across the north of England to secure their empire from the hostile tribes of southern Scotland. Even after they built the Antonine Wall around AD 145, between Old Kilpatrick on the River Clyde and Bo'ness on the River Forth, the Romans occupied the south of Scotland intermittently. Glasgow's Hunterian Museum and Edinburgh's National Museum of Scotland have interesting displays on the Antonine Wall, and you can see remains of the wall by walking the 60km (37 miles) Antonine Way.

The Antonine Wall was a turf rampart,
up to four metres high, fronted by a deep ditch.

The Land of the Celts

Kilmartin Glen, near the Crinan Canal in the southwest Highlands, is an impressive ritual landscape, studded with chambered cairns, stone circles, standing stones and a coronation hill. This was the capital territory of Dal Riata, the kingdom of Celtic tribes known as the Scotii, which gave their name to all of Scotland. Dunadd Hill, the coronation place of their kings, and the many burial mounds and stone monuments show the glen's importance in the history of this country. You can unlock the secrets of Scotland's Valley of the Kings at the Kilmartin House Museum in Kilmartin village.

There are more than 350 ancient monuments in Kilmartin Glen.

Celtic Christianity

St Ninian, whose mission to Scotland
was based in Candida Casa (the 'white
house') in Whithorn, Galloway, brought
Christianity to the southern Picts in the 4th
century. St Columba, from his base on Iona,
evangelised the northern Picts in the 6th
century. Both were leading figures in the
Celtic Church, which is traditionally seen as
more spiritual and more inclusive of women
than Roman Catholicism. The cities and
towns of Scotland still have their own
patron saints. For example, Edinburgh has
St Cuthbert, Perth has St John the Baptist,
Aberdeen has St Nicholas, Paisley has St
Mirren and Dumfries has St Michael.

*St Ninian at Whithorn. The roofless edifice on the left is
the ruined chapel on the 'Isle' of Whithorn (a peninsula).*

The Lands of the Picts

The Aberlemno Sculptured Stones are
among the small number of artefacts
left behind by the Pictish tribes who
inhabited the north and east of Scotland.
The five stones, in the Angus village of
the same name, are inscribed with a wide
range of Pictish symbols, and date from
around AD 800. The Sculptured Stone
Museum, in the Perthshire village of
Meigle, where 26 Pictish stones are on
display, explains the history of the Pictish
people and the meaning of the carvings.
Kenneth MacAlpin united the Scots and
Picts as one nation in AD 843, which
was the beginning of a united Scotland.

*Visit Aberlemno in summer if you can: the stones are
protected by wooden boxes in the winter months.*

The Vikings

Up Helly Aa, a fire festival held on the last Tuesday in January every year, takes the people of Lerwick, the capital of Shetland, back to their Viking roots. This spectacular event includes torch-light processions through the town, which end in the burning of a Norse galley, followed by a night of music and entertainment. During the rest of the year, a visit to the many Viking sites in Shetland and Orkney, such as the burial chamber at Maeshowe, can be just as inspiring. Tankerness House Museum, in Kirkwall, Orkney, and the Shetland Museum in Lerwick, tell the story of 5,000 years of island life.

The Viking raids were by no means confined to Shetland and Orkney. Iona was attacked in AD 795, 802 and 806.

Norse Connections

Vikings raided and then settled on the northern and western coasts of Scotland, between AD 700 and 1200, and their language and culture have become embedded in many place names (such as Dingwall) and common Scots words (such as oose and haar). The Lewis Chessmen, found in 1831, were probably made in Norway in the 12th century. The Battle of Largs in 1263, an important conflict in freeing western Scotland from Viking rule, is celebrated in that Ayrshire town every October, with a re-enactment of the battle, fireworks and the ceremonial burning of a longboat.

The Lewis Chessmen were carved in walrus ivory and whales' teeth; they were found buried in the sand.

The Wars of Independence

The Battle of Bannockburn, Scotland's most significant victory in the first War of Scottish Independence, was fought on 23rd and 24th June 1314 on rough ground just south of Stirling. Although greatly outnumbered by the English under King Edward II, the Scottish army led by Robert the Bruce won a convincing victory, thanks to their agility and innovative tactics. During the closely fought contest, the English knights on horses couldn't get through the Scottish schiltrons – defensive 'huddles' of soldiers brandishing spears – and so 'proud Edward' II was sent homeward, to think again. The Bannockburn Heritage Centre tells the story.

The battle features in the chorus of 'Flower of Scotland', the unofficial national anthem.

The Declaration of Arbroath

Bannockburn may have been a famous Scottish victory, but the country was fearful of another invasion by its southern neighbour. So on 6 April 1320, a group of 39 Scottish nobles sent the Declaration of Arbroath to Pope John XXII, confirming the country's independence and their willingness to defend it to the death. The most famous passage reads: 'It is in truth not for glory, nor riches, nor honours that we are fighting, but for freedom – for that alone, which no honest man gives up but with life itself.' A copy of the declaration is held by the National Archives of Scotland, Edinburgh.

The Declaration of Arbroath inspired the wording of the American Declaration of Independence.

The Scottish Reformation

John Knox, who was born in Haddington in 1514, trained as a priest before converting to the Calvinist cause at the age of 40. He became the public face of the Scottish Reformation, which in 1560 dismantled the Roman Catholic Church in Scotland and replaced it with a Protestant national church, the Church of Scotland, headed by God and not the Pope. The St Mungo Museum of Religious Life and Art in Glasgow, the first museum of religions in the world, presents day-to-day life for the followers of the six largest religions in the world (Buddhism, Christianity, Hinduism, Islam, Judaism and Sikhism).

John Knox House, in the Netherbow on Edinburgh's Royal Mile, is now home to the Scottish Storytelling Centre.

Mary, Queen of Scots

When Mary, Queen of Scots, arrived
from France in 1561 to claim the Scottish
throne, she found a very different country
to the one she had left as a child. Mary, a
Roman Catholic, stepped into a country
that had embraced the Reformation and
was now Protestant in its religious views.
She was tolerant of the reformed church,
but the Reformers forced her to abdicate in
favour of her son, James VI, which began
a civil war that ended with the Reformers
triumphant. Mary, forced into exile in
England, was captured and executed by
Queen Elizabeth I, who suspected a Roman
Catholic plot to overthrow her.

*Imprisoned for almost 19 years, Mary is often portrayed
writing, but some of 'her' letters were probably forged.*

The Witch Trials

Witchcraft was a criminal offence between 1563 and 1736, and punishable by death. During those years, more than 3,500 people, most of them women, were accused under the Scottish Witchcraft Act of 1563, and 1,500 were found guilty and executed. Most convictions resulted from forced confessions, usually made after sleep deprivation and other forms of torture. There is a small memorial, at the entrance to the esplanade of Edinburgh Castle, to the alleged witches who were put to death in the capital. There is also a Witches Maze at Tullibole Castle, Perthshire, where 11 people were put to death in 1662.

Most of those convicted of witchcraft in Scotland were strangled or hanged and then burnt in public.

Union with England

Scotland's wars of independence and religion ended in 1603 when James VI of Scotland was invited to become James I of England. Scotland may have won peace and Protestantism, but the Royal Court – the source of power and patronage – left Edinburgh for London. The Scottish Parliament remained, however, until the Union of the Parliaments in 1707, which saw power transferred again to London. Scotland, however, was guaranteed independence on religion, law and education. Parliament House, the home of the first Scottish Parliament, now houses the Supreme Courts of Scotland.

The first Union Flag, combining the flags of Scotland and England, was designed by James VI and I.

The Jacobite Rebellions

Supporters of James Stuart (the Old Pretender) and his son Charles (the Young Pretender, better known as Bonnie Prince Charlie), made the last attempt to put a Catholic monarch on the British throne. The most important risings were in 1715, under James, and in 1745, under Charles. The '45 rising began in August when Charles arrived in Scotland from France. Gathering supporters as he went, he headed for London. He was defeated at Derby in December, and began a retreat. The final battle was at Culloden, near Inverness, in April 1746, when the Jacobites were soundly beaten. The Culloden Visitor Centre tells the story.

'Speed, bonnie boat…' The prince's crossing to Skye was from Benbecula, on North Uist, rather than the mainland.

Clearance and Exile

The Clearances, when the aristocratic landlords of the Highlands and Islands forced their tenants from the land to make way for sheep farms and sporting estates, devastated the culture of the north of Scotland in the 18th and 19th centuries. The evocative 'Exiles' statue in Helsmdale, Sutherland, where the worst of the Clearances took place, and the ruins of many abandoned villages remind the modern visitor of the fate of the hundreds of thousands who were forced abroad. Now, around 40 million people around the world claim Scots descent, eight times the population of the country itself.

The 'Exiles' statue in Helmsdale. There's an identical one in Winnipeg, Canada, where many Scots went.

A Scientific Enlightenment

The Scottish Enlightenment, which began
in the 1750s, revolutionised scientific, social
and intellectual activities. It substituted
logic and rationality for tradition and
superstition, and promoted education
and debate. In science, James Hutton
pioneered geology, Joseph Black formalised
chemistry and William Cullen founded
modern medicine. Their contributions
were practical and useful, not simply
philosophical. This was because the leading
figures in Scotland's four universities mixed
with people in commerce and industry in
a number of learned societies, so that their
ideas reflected the real world.

*'Hutton's Unconformity' refers to rock formations at various
sites, the best-known being at Siccar Point, Berwickshire.*

A Practical Enlightenment

The three giants of the Scottish Enlightenment – David Hume, Adam Smith and Thomas Reid – pioneered not only new ways of thinking, but their practical application to the modern world. Hume developed what we now call the scientific method, Smith the science of economics, and Reid what is called Common Sense philosophy. Their books and ideas remain relevant. Smith's classic *Wealth of Nations* (1776) is still one of the most influential books ever published, and all three thinkers had an effect on the founders of the emerging nation of America. The monument to David Hume is a highlight of Old Calton cemetery in Edinburgh.

Adam Smith penned great works on philosophy and economics. He was brilliant but, it's said, rather absent-minded.

A Wider Enlightenment

The third strand of the Scottish Enlightenment was the spread of knowledge, through education and through books and journals. William Smellie, a friend of Robert Burns, edited the first edition of the *Encyclopaedia Britannica*, which was published in Edinburgh in 100 weekly instalments from 1768, then re-issued in three volumes. Also in Edinburgh, William Chambers and Algernon Blackwood published journals bearing their name, which attracted the most prominent writers in Britain, and circulated internationally. The Writers' Museum in Edinburgh celebrates the city's authors and publishers.

The first Britannica was in three volumes; the 2010 edition, the last to appear in print, runs to 32 volumes.

The Industrial Revolution

The great leaps forward of the Enlightenment meant Scotland was ripe for development, and the Industrial Revolution here powered Britain's imperial expansion during the Victorian era. Mining, shipbuilding, iron and steel production – along with the creation of an extensive railway and canal network – all transformed Scotland beyond recognition during the 19th century. Those days of heavy industry are now gone, but the 22-acre Summerlee Museum of Scottish Industrial Life in Lanarkshire allows visitors to experience the vanished coal mines, foundries, mills and engineering industries, and to learn about the lives of those who worked there.

Steel-making is not just hot work: Summerlee has the distinction of being Scotland's noisiest museum.

Pioneering and Exploration

The Industrial Revolution brought new opportunities in the daredevil world of exploration. Mungo Park, from Foulshiels in the Borders, was the first Westerner to reach the Niger River in West Africa. Lanarkshire's David Livingstone opened up vast tracts of southern and central Africa, making him a huge celebrity for the Victorians, and he was buried in Westminster Abbey, London. As well as the Tropics, Scots explored the polar regions. John Rae, from Orkney, was a highly skilled cold-climate specialist and spent years in the frozen North. He finally solved the riddle of the (in)famous Franklin Expedition, lost nearly a decade before, in the 1840s.

Harold Raeburn was mountaineering leader on the 1921 British Everest expedition. He learned his skills on Ben Nevis.

Oil, Gas and Renewables

Exploration was key to the discovery of substantial oil and gas reserves in the North Sea in the late 1960s, which made Aberdeen a world-class energy capital, known as the Dallas of Europe. As well as these hydrocarbon fuels, Scotland has – as visitors will tell you – an inexhaustible supply of wind and water. These sources of renewable energy have inspired a new wave of innovative technologies to capture wind, hydro and tidal power and transmit it efficiently to where it is needed. The visitor centre in Cruachan Power Station, near Oban, explains how turbines extract power from fast-flowing water.

Around a quarter of Europe's total energy resources are in, or under, Scottish waters.

Home Rule: 1979 Referendum

The issue of Home Rule (devolution, not independence) for Scotland gathered momentum from the 1920s on. One of the most visible events was the repatriation of the Stone of Destiny from Westminster Abbey on Christmas Day in 1951 by a group of nationalist students. The stone had been taken from Scotland in 1296 by Edward I of England and placed in the Coronation Chair. The political culmination of the Home Rule movement was a referendum in 1979, which returned a small majority for devolution. However, fewer than the stipulated 40 per cent of the electorate voted for change, and the status quo prevailed.

According to one tradition, the stone was previously used as Jacob's Pillow, mentioned in the Biblical Book of Genesis.

Parliament and Independence

The demand for devolution would not go away, and in 1997 Scots were given another chance to vote on the issue. A decisive 74.3% approved the creation of a Scottish Parliament. The elections for the new body took place in May 1999, and the new Scottish Executive, with Labour's Donald Dewar as First Minister, took power. The new Scottish Parliament Building was opened in 2004. The SNP, which gained majority power in 2011, made good on their promise for a referendum on independence. It was held on 18th September 2014, with 45% voting in favour and 55% against. The biggest triumph was the 84.6% turnout, the highest recorded in the UK since universal suffrage.

The Scottish Parliament building was designed by Catalan architect Enric Miralles.

SCOTIA'S GRANDEUR

There's not just one Scotland, there are many. That may sound a little strange, but it's undeniably true. The local history, the landscapes and even the language change mile by mile, as you exchange the rolling hills of the Borders for the modern, post-industrial Central Belt, home to Glasgow and Edinburgh.

It remains true as you leave the crowded waistline of the country and head for the picturesque east coast, historic Perthshire and the extraordinary mountains of the Highlands. And it is a very obvious truth indeed when you surrender dry land and discover the many and varied islands of the north and west.

In short, there are as many Scotlands as you could wish for. And 'Scotia's grandeur' – to borrow a phrase from Burns' poem 'The Cotter's Saturday Night' – is truly a sight to behold. Where else in the world can you see majestic mountains and historic castles rising from green, misty glens? Where else do medieval wynds sit alongside modern marvels of engineering? And where else do picturesque harbours, unspoilt beaches and beautiful lochs lie a short stroll from mysterious standing stones or world-famous golf links?

The middle of the country – towns and cities such as Stirling, Callander, Perth and Dunkeld – witnessed some of the key moments in Scottish history, whilst southern settlements such as Berwick-upon-Tweed, Duns, Jedburgh, Peebles and Selkirk are testament to centuries of raids back and forth over the border with England.

With more cultural and arts centres than anywhere else of remotely comparable size, and more wilderness than the most intrepid of us could ever fully explore in one lifetime, Scotland has a myriad of braw places just waiting to be discovered – all in one friendly wee country.

Glasgow

Scotland's biggest city is feisty, friendly and fun – it's 'miles better', according to the old promotional campaign. Designated as the European Capital of Culture in 1990, this industrial city has had a renaissance in recent decades: world-class architecture includes the medieval cathedral, Mackintosh design and cutting-edge new structures. A breeding ground for contemporary artists and with a thriving music scene, Glasgow is also home to the ballet and opera, and bustling boutiques make it a shopper's paradise. The world's first football international (Scotland v England) was held in Glasgow in 1872, and the Old Firm rivalry between Celtic and Rangers is legendary.

Best-known for its early 20th-century 'Glasgow Style', the city's architectural highlights span several centuries.

The Clyde Waterfront

Victorian Glasgow was the 'Second City
of the British Empire': it grew big and
prosperous as a centre for heavy industry,
and as shipbuilder and engineer to the world.
But in the space of a few decades in the
postwar period, the economic rug was pulled,
leaving Weegies with the task of redefining
themselves. And where better to witness their
reinvention than the new Clyde Waterfront?
A series of prestige projects – including the
Science Centre, the 'Squinty Bridge' (Clyde
Arc), the Clyde Auditorium, the digital
media quarter on Pacific Quay and the
Riverside Museum – point the way towards
an even brighter future.

*Old meets new where the 'Tall Ship' is berthed alongside
the Riverside Museum, designed by Zaha Hadid.*

Edinburgh

The nation's capital may be smaller than Glasgow, but Edinburgh's aspirations are a match for any metropolis. Not content with being the 'Athens of the North', this city of festivals could be the London, the Cannes, the Montreux. Indeed, where else in the world can you experience every conceivable form of stage entertainment in such magnificent surroundings? Dominated by the dramatic Castle, the Royal Mile positively oozes history, while centuries of writing prompted UNESCO to designate this the first ever City of Literature. Natural history can be enjoyed at the Botanic Garden, Zoo and Dynamic Earth, and then there's the National Museum and array of art collections.

Once part of the majestic castle's defences, Princes Street Gardens were created by draining Nor Loch.

The Scottish Parliament

Holyrood, the central Edinburgh location for Scotland's legislative home, is historic yet modern in every sense. Enric Miralles' adventurous design for the building, completed in 2004, references natural themes from landscape to leaves, and cultural highlights too, such as Henry Raeburn's Skating Minister painting. A light-filled structure designed for sustainability, this landmark embodies Scotland's national dream. And inside its walls – whether of granite, oak or glass – the political process is a model of modern democracy, with a proportional representation system designed to best reflect the views of the citizens it serves.

The Parliament building's organic design was intended to mirror and blend with its natural surroundings.

Leith

From *Trainspotting* to BMW-watching, Edinburgh's port has something for everyone, not least for lovers of wine bars, bistros and bijou flats. This is no newly established community, however. Serving the city since medieval times, the historic port was more than a place for sailors and cargo: it was once home to the Scottish Court; it provided a defensive frontline against invaders from all quarters; and it is even the 'true' home of golf, the place where this most Scottish of sports was codified in a series of rules that still stand today. No doubt, then, that Leith has earned the honour of becoming the Royal Yacht Britannia's permanent home.

Who would not walk 500 miles to enjoy the sunshine on Leith's waterfront?

The Forth Bridge

You can keep your Golden Gate, your
Brooklyn, your Sydney Harbour ...
Scotland has the world's most iconic
bridge, bar none. Not the Forth Road
Bridge, you understand, nor the
Queensferry Crossing, currently under
construction. No, we're talking Sir John
Fowler and Sir Benjamin Baker's railway
crossing, now a UNESCO World Heritage
site. By the time it was opened in 1890, all
this 2.5km (1.5 miles) bridge needed was
a lick of red paint. Notoriously, they were
still applying that throughout the 20th
century. By the end of 2011, they were
finally done. For the time being, anyway.

*This landmark boasts the world's second-longest
single cantilever bridge span.*

The Falkirk Wheel

A canal system built two centuries ago that
is now crowded with cabin cruisers and
narrow boats putt-putt-puttering along:
it may not seem the most Space-Age
of settings. Yet it's here, in a basin just
outside Falkirk, that our high-tech, low-
carbon future is displayed. The world's first
rotating boat lift raises and lowers vessels in
a giant moveable lock between the Union
and Forth & Clyde canals. The gondolas
hold enough water to fill an Olympic
swimming pool, yet almost all the work
of the 24-metre height change is done by
gravity. Ingenious! And it's a mere paddle
along the canal from the Kelpies.

*It takes just 5 minutes and 30 seconds
for a boat to complete its 180° passage.*

Stirling

One of several self-proclaimed 'gateways to the Highlands', Stirling is much more interesting in its own right as one of Scotland's most historic and attractive cities. Some 700 years have passed since it played its starring role in the Wars of Independence – when both William Wallace and Robert the Bruce sent the English fleeing south – but the 'Royal Burgh' still has all the old charisma. The castle on its crag; the medieval buildings beneath its walls; the Victorian Gothic of the towering memorial to Scotland's 'Braveheart': stroll through Stirling and you're walking into history.

'Freedom!' The imposing Wallace Monument has 264 steps and a 'hall of fame' with busts of patriotic heroes.

Doune

The Gaelic word *dun* means 'fort': there's
been a stronghold here since prehistoric
times. The one we see today was built in
the 14th century and featured extensively in
the movie *Monty Python and the Holy Grail*.
Doune Castle has since been the centre of
another medieval resurrection: the pilgrimage.
Python devotees flock here from every corner
of the world, along with fans of the historical
time travel novels and TV series *Outlander*, in
which the castle has a starring role as 'Castle
Leoch'. A pistol factory was set up in Doune
in the 17th century, and a Doune pistol is said
to have fired the first shot of the American
War of Independence.

*Robert Spittal reputedly built the Bridge of Teith
in 1535 after being refused passage by the ferryman.*

East Neuk

'Classy in a soft-spoken, east-of-Scotland kind of way.' That was the *Guardian*'s verdict on the East Neuk Festival. The same could be said for the East Neuk as a whole – although this only begins to sum up the allure of the southeast corner of the Kingdom of Fife. The picturesque villages clustered along this stretch of coastline near St Andrews feature stone-built fishermen's cottages, manors and churches overlooking the historic harbours. Linked by the Fife Coastal Path, these settlements make the perfect destination for holidaymakers who seek tranquillity and charm.

As well as a harbour for the daily catch, historic Crail boasts one of the world's oldest golf courses.

Dundee

In the City of Discovery you can explore
the RRS *Discovery*, which carried Scott
and Shackleton's team to the Antarctic
(1901–4). The venerable vessel has a new
waterfront neighbour: the V&A Dundee.
Scotland's favourite family, the Broons, may
live in Auchenshoogle, but their creators are
Dundee-based D C Thomson, whose stable
of pure cartoon genius also includes the *Beano*
and *Dandy*. Grown-up Dundonians can
forge a career in computer games: Abertay
University is a world-class centre. The city's
original university plays host to the UK's
most established mountain film festival and a
thriving literature festival.

The Waterfront complex is transforming the skyline:
iconic new structures nestle alongside more familiar ones.

The Cairngorms

The vast and incredibly beautiful Highland region in the northeast of the country represents perfect postcard Scotland. Starting from Perthshire's gateway resort towns, Aberfeldy and Pitlochry, with all their old-world charm, you can experience the rugged splendour of the mountains and nature in Cairngorms National Park. Aviemore and Glenshee are the places to head if skiing is your thing, while cultural events take place year-round in historic Speyside, which is also home to some of Scotland's finest whisky distilleries. With so much to see and do, it's little wonder that this part of Scotland is the destination of choice for the Queen, at Balmoral Castle and Royal Deeside.

Winter wonderland: conditions in Scotland's high ground provide exhilarating skiing and ice-climbing for the intrepid.

Aberdeen

The Aberdeen story is a tale of two cities, Old and New – but bear in mind that 'New' Aberdeen got that title in the 14th century. The Granite City was transformed in the 1970s by the discovery of 'black gold' in the North Sea, and the energy capital is now taking a lead in the move from oil to renewables, like waves and wind-power: green energy. Green's the word at the BBC's popular *Beechgrove Garden* TV programme, too, which gives gardening tips to the nation. A thriving cultural life is celebrated in the International Youth Festival, where more than 30,000 people enjoy arts events in the long, light days of summer.

A Granite Festival celebrates the city's heritage with fascinating exhibitions and talks.

Inverness

A city since 2001, Inverness has been an important centre since Pictish times, and there's been a castle on the hill since the 11th century. Mary, Queen of Scots sought sanctuary here in 1562 but was denied, making this one of the few Scottish castles in which she *didn't* spend a night. Today, Inverness is much more welcoming: it's the fastest growing city – not just in Scotland but in western Europe, thanks to its expanding economy and top-rated quality of life. An ideal base for exploring history and nature, the area also jumps to the beat of RockNess and the family-friendly Tartan Heart Festival, at nearby Belladrum.

The first Inverness Castle was where Shakespeare's Macbeth committed murder; the new castle is now a Sheriff's Court.

John o' Groats

In spite of popular belief, this windswept village is not the mainland's most northerly point: that distinction belongs to nearby Dunnet Head. Nevertheless, visitors galore turn up here for a photo opportunity before removing themselves as far away as possible by making the 1,407-kilometre (874-mile) journey to Land's End – because this is the farthest distance between two inhabited points on the UK mainland. If you've just cycled or walked all the way up from Cornwall and are at your journey's end, then you're sure to find this the most beautiful place on earth.

Dutchman Jan de Groot gave his name to this spot when he set up the Orkney ferry landing in 1496.

JOHN O'GROATS

Orkney and Shetland

As far as many of their inhabitants are
concerned, these northern isles aren't in
Scotland at all – except in the most pallid
technical and administrative senses. There's
certainly quite a contrast between
low-lying Orkney, with its big green fields,
and the rugged Highland scenery – though
the same could be said of Caithness,
its immediate mainland neighbour.
The Shetlands are wilder, their people
traditionally directed more to fishing than
to agriculture. Both island groups were
settled by Vikings and for several centuries,
politically and culturally, looked east to
Scandinavia rather than south to Scotland.

*Orkney's Ring of Brodgar was once known as the
Temple of the Sun: in June, it can be sunny for 18 hours!*

St Kilda

Technically, this little island group belongs to the Outer Hebrides, though it's farther west from Lewis (73km or 45 miles) than Lewis is from the mainland. So isolated is St Kilda, indeed, that it has its own distinct subspecies: a St Kilda woodmouse and a St Kilda wren. Ancient sheep breeds are also found: feral now, since the human inhabitants who for so many centuries scratched a living here were evacuated in 1930. It's a melancholy place today, though the abandoned cottages complement the ruins of earlier medieval and prehistoric settlements in this most atmospheric of Scottish isles.

Milder winters have caused St Kilda's brown Soay sheep to become smaller since scientists began studying them.

Lewis and Harris

Confusingly, Lewis and Harris are actually a single island – the largest off Scotland's coast. An isthmus between East and West Loch Tarbert separates North Harris from South Harris, but Lewis begins further to the north, between Lochs Seaforth and Resort. To make matters more perplexing, 'Harris' tweed is produced in both Lewis and Harris (and, indeed, the Outer Hebrides at large). But some things are reassuringly simple here, especially on Sundays, when more or less everything is closed for the traditional day of rest. All the better to view the outstanding beauty of the scenery, from unspoilt beaches to cliffs, moors, hillsides and lochs.

The megaliths at Callanish include a giant cross-shaped arrangement; Lewis has many other standing stones, too.

Isle of Skye

Small enough to be manageable and yet large enough to get lost in, the Isle of Skye is its own little world, a place apart. It's also a scenic paradise with its Black Cuillin, its Red Hills, its moors and bogs and its craggy coastline, a playground for climbers, birdwatchers and walkers. You can drive there too, without queuing hours for the ferry, since the old pretenders of Maggie Thatcher's government composed a new Skye Bridge Song ('Over the Sea by PFI…'). And it's free: tolls were dropped in 2004 after a furious campaign. Skye's name is derived from the Old Norse for 'cloudy island'; the largest town, Portree, is from the Gaelic for 'king's port'.

The magnificent Cuillins viewed from Elgol. The Cuillin Ridge Traverse is the UK's toughest mountain challenge.

Eilean Donan

It's an iconic scene: the romantic castle
on its little island, connected to shore by
a quaint-looking footbridge, reflected
in the glassy waters; a tranquil landscape
that seems almost too picturesque to be
true. The famous castle is, indeed, not all
it seems, built between 1912 and 1932.
But it *was* built from the rubble of a real
medieval castle, which protected against
Norse invasions and had seen historic
action as recently as 1719. A Spanish
task force landed Jacobite rebels here.
Capturing the castle, they set out to
conquer Scotland for the Stuarts, only to
be defeated at Glen Shiel.

The castle stands on the site of a church
built by Donnán of Eigg, the martyred Celtic saint.

Glenfinnan Viaduct

It sometimes seems that you can hardly
walk into a cinema or switch on the
television without seeing this magnificent
viaduct – as featured most famously
in the Harry Potter films. Even so, it
is impressive to see it 'in the flesh':
engineering becomes art in the effortless
sweep of this structure, its 21 arches
striding spectacularly across the glen.
Below, a little way down the glen, on
a patch of boggy ground beside Loch
Shiel, a monument marks the spot where
the Jacobites raised their standard when
Bonnie Prince Charles landed here at the
start of the ill-fated '45.

The Jacobite train on the famously scenic West Highland
Line, which connects Fort William and Mallaig.

Loch Ness

Britain's second largest loch by surface area
(after Loch Lomond) and the second deepest
(after Loch Morar). Loch Ness has the greatest
volume of water – and, amazingly, contains
more water than all the lakes of England
and Wales combined. Long and straight (in
keeping with its situation along the line of
the Caledonian Fault), it has just one island,
Cherry Island, which is a crannog, created near
the southern shore during the Iron Age. The
loch's most noteworthy feature, of course, is
the monster – and what an amazing attraction
that is, whether it be living plesiosaur, mass-
hysterical mirage or simply myth. What else
could any expanse of water need?

*Urquhart Castle's earliest incarnation dates back as far as the
6th century; perhaps St Columba glimpsed Nessie here?*

Ben Nevis

Standing just outside Fort William
in Lochaber, Britain's highest
mountain is impressive both in bulk
and height: Ben Nevis rises 1,344m
(4,409ft) above sea level. Up here,
you have to readjust your ideas of the
Highlands as a sanctuary of peace.
The 'pony track' to the summit is as
busy as Buchanan Street in summer:
over 100,000 ascents are made each
year. Serious climbers come up
by rockier routes – or wait for the
winter ice and snow to make it more
'interesting'. There's something for
every adventurer on Ben Nevis.

*Despite the effort required to scale the heights,
solitude is rare at the summit of our highest mountain.*

Ardnamurchan

The westernmost place on the UK mainland lies 35km (22 miles) farther west than Land's End. It is perhaps the most unspoilt, too – though Scotland is spoilt for choice in unspoilt spots. Remote it may be, but Ardnamurchan Point is well known to listeners of the Met Office's shipping forecast. The weather statistics around here might surprise you, in fact. Despite the gales and storms, it's just a few miles from Tiree, the most westerly isle of the Inner Hebrides, with its famous (and unlikely) claim to be the sunniest place in Britain. In 2011, a 1,000-year-old Viking chieftain's burial ship with all its treasures was discovered at Ardnamurchan.

Ardnamurchan means 'headland of the great seas'. Wild as it is, there are glorious sheltered beaches here too.

Mull and Iona

One of the largest of the Inner Hebrides, Mull is also among the loveliest, a popular destination for sealife cruises and tourist trips. The delightful little fishing port of Tobermory is loaded with significance for lovers of children's TV: it was the setting for *Balamory* and the name of a Womble in the '70s series. Iona, off Mull's southwestern tip, was where in AD 563 the Irish exile St Columba set up his monastery: since the 1930s the Iona Community has continued to worship in the restored abbey. Macbeth is one of many Scottish kings buried here, and the Book of Kells was probably created here too. Nearby Staffa has intriguing basalt columns and the impressive Fingal's Cave.

Tobermory, meaning 'Mary's well' in Gaelic, is known for its brightly painted waterfront buildings.

Glencoe

How far it is history and how far simply the scenery – stark and dramatic – it's hard to say, but this deep glen can seem as full of foreboding as it is of beauty. It was in February 1692 that a party of Campbell troops enlisted in the cause of King William III (William II of Scotland) fell upon the MacDonalds on whom they had been billeted. Clan rivalry and politics prompted the infamous massacre, which left 38 dead. Another 40 – mostly women and children – driven from their homes, perished in the snow. Today, however, the majesty of the mountains draws visitors aplenty, whether passing through along the West Highland Way or lingering to climb, camp or simply admire the stunning views.

Mountaineers aren't the only people who'll recognise this scenery: one of the Harry Potter films was shot here.

Loch Lomond

Whichever road you tak' to get there,
don't miss Loch Lomond, Scotland's largest
freshwater loch (by surface area) – and for
some, the most beautiful into the bargain.
Certainly it is the most celebrated (Loch Ness
is notorious – not quite the same): what other
area of open water was ever so memorably
summed up in song? Visitors flock here in
the summer, but it's surprisingly easy to find
peace, gazing out across Loch Lomond's open
waters – an astonishing expanse of azure,
studded with islands, sparkling emeralds of
green. Beyond Ben Lomond, on the eastern
shore, lie the rugged mountains and wooded
glens of the Trossachs.

*Ben Lomond (Gaelic for 'Beacon Mountain'), on the
eastern 'bonnie bank', is the most southerly Munro.*

Arran

Tucked in between the Ayrshire coast
and the long, jagged finger of Kintyre,
Arran is a natural haven for plants and
birds, rare mammals and marine life. It's
also a geologist's paradise as it's divided
by the Highland Boundary Fault and is a
place of quite astonishing scenic beauty.
As elsewhere in the Highlands and Islands,
though, the enchanting sense of solitude and
peace was cruelly come by in the Clearances
of the early 19th century, when hundreds
of families were expelled to free up grazing
land. There are still sheep to be seen here,
but Arran is not to be confused with the
Irish sweater-source, the Aran Islands.

*Arran is known as 'Scotland in Miniature' because
of its contrasting Highland and Lowland areas.*

Mull of Kintyre

As the crow flies, it's closer to Belfast than to Glasgow; mainland Antrim is just 20km (12 miles) across the North Channel, but this is the end of the road – and the end of the world, it sometimes feels. Paul McCartney's desire may have been always to be here, but the Liverpool-born bard wasn't making up the bit about the 'mist rolling in from the sea', and the prospect of being marooned here by the fog isn't always inviting. Little wonder that one of Scotland's earliest lighthouses was commissioned on the treacherous headland.

But when the sun struggles out, this is a place of peace and spellbinding beauty, and a wildlife-watcher's Arcadia.

Wings over the mull: the winds aren't suitable for paragliding, and it's rarely sunny – but you can dream!

Alloway

Not too far from better-known
Galloway, this village (now more or less
a part of Ayr) is the celebrated birthplace
of Robert Burns. The cottage in which
Scotland's Bard was born (in 1759) is
now part of a state-of-the-art museum.

It was in Alloway that our national
poet went to school and worked as a
farm labourer; here he courted his first
girlfriends and wrote his first poems.

Alloway has a major role in 'Tam
o'Shanter' as it's where Tam sits drinking
late at the start of the classic poem – and
goes on to witness warlocks and witches
in a dance at the town's Auld Kirk.

Just in time before the fearsome witches catch up,
Meg speeds Tam across the Brig o' Doon into Alloway.

Gretna

In Scotland – but only just – this Dumfriesshire village started attracting English couples in 1753. That year's Marriage Act forced under-21s in England to get parental permission before they wed. But just over the border, young lovers could still plight their troth without interference; an adventurer could 'steal an heiress' and know that he'd be safe here from English law. Since all you needed was a witness, the local blacksmith did the honours: the old forge remains a romantic shrine, and the anvil a symbol of marriage. Visitors flock to the village to see 'murmurations' of thousands of starlings flying in mesmerising formations.

Scotland to the left,
England to the right…

The Borders

This was never the easiest part of Scotland
to pin down, as the plural 'Borders' perhaps
suggests; in the west, for a while, these were
the 'Debatable Lands'. The historical reality
wasn't quite that sedate, however. 'Reiving'
– raiding – back and forth across the border
was a way of life for centuries. Today, by
contrast, all is calm and quiet – a tranquillity
perhaps typified by Abbotsford, the romantic
home of Sir Walter Scott. This region
of historic burghs, of enchanting rolling
hills and rocky coastlines, with the Tweed
snaking through, gives little of its turbulent
past away, except in its picturesque ruins,
such as that of Melrose Abbey.

*Visitors to the Borders find themselves in an ideal place
for outdoor pursuits, from mountain biking to birding.*

New Lanark

This 18th-century cotton mill village is
now a World Heritage site and tribute to
the Industrial Revolution, but it was also
something of a revolution in itself. It was
here that reformer Robert Owen showed
that a worker's life – though never, perhaps,
positively enjoyable – didn't actually have
to be a hell on earth. He provided his
staff with clean and properly maintained
accommodation and set up schools for the
education of their children. And, much to the
amazement of his fellow-industrialists, he still
made money. They were impressed – as are
the 400,000 tourists and schoolchildren who
visit this unique town/museum annually.

The New Lanark project was founded by David Dale,
Robert Owen's father-in-law, in 1786.

ILKA JOY
AND TREASURE

'Flower of Scotland', the unofficial national anthem, is sung with pride on special occasions and evokes this country's unique culture and traditions. The skirl of the pipes, tartan kilts, shortbread and the Loch Ness monster: they are all Scottish icons recognised the world over. As are the thistle and the stag, gorgeous textiles such as Harris Tweed and Fair Isle knitwear, and the raucous dancing of a classic ceilidh.

And let's not forget Robert Louis Stevenson, Sir Walter Scott, Sir Arthur Conan Doyle. Architects such as Charles Rennie Mackintosh, artists such as the Glasgow Boys. Castles, crofting and shipbuilding. The luxurious pleasure of a wee dram of malt whisky. For centuries, Scotland has been home to 'ilka [every] joy and treasure', to quote the Bard, from his poem 'Ae Fond Kiss'.

These symbols of Scotland in days gone by still very much have their place, but this is a country that's also embraced the 21st century. And in this modern, sophisticated land, the old traditions have certainly not held back the development of a vibrant new culture. In fact, they often go hand in hand.

The old universities now rank alongside the best in the world, and the same goes for the links courses hosting the ancient game of golf. Even Scotland's traditional foods have been updated into delicious contemporary dishes, whilst our fresh seafood is shipped around the world.

Scotland continues to produce global cultural icons: sports stars, artists, musicians, authors, film stars and computer games designers. And as hosts of major events, from the Commonwealth Games to the greatest New Year's Eve party in the world (bar none), Scots have proved themselves to be endlessly hospitable. It's just the way we are – it's a part of the culture.

Crofting

Small-scale food production in crofting communities is part of Scotland's rural fabric, yet only since 1886 have crofters been guaranteed security of tenure. Traditionally, they grew vegetables and grazed cattle communally, fertilising the thin soils with nutrient-rich seaweed, and laboriously cutting peat to burn as fuel. The soggy Highland and Island bogs are full of grasses, which eventually decay and, as successive layers accumulate, they are composted and compressed, forming peat. On Islay, peat fires used to dry the malt confer the whisky's distinctive flavour. Today, there are around 17,000 crofts, modernised and sustainably run.

Aside from the traditional use of peat as a heat source, peat bogs protect against flooding and host diverse wildlife.

Ceilidhs and Music

The national sound of Scotland is the bagpipe,
a combination of an air-supply blowstick, a
bag, a chanter (or melody pipe) and at least one
drone, which produces a constant harmonising
note. The pipes were once used as substitutes
for trumpets on the battlefield, and pipe bands
remained a big part of the Scottish military, as
well as performing at weddings and other national
events today. But it's usually a combination
of fiddler, accordionist and perhaps a whistler,
drummer or other traditional instrumentalist that
comprise the classic ceilidh band, belting out the
Gay Gordons, Strip the Willow and other tunes
for an energetic, often multi-generational crowd
to dance the night awa'.

The Scots know how to party, and all are welcome to join in!
The ceilidh is a mainstay of Burns Suppers, weddings and more.

Clash of the Tartans

The kilt was worn in the 16th century as a plaid cloth draped over the body and belted. Around a century later, it had been adapted into the 'walking' kilt: a cloth woven in a distinctive clan pattern, pleated and fashioned like a skirt. This is the style that remains popular today. But in the wake of the Jacobite rebellions, wearing the kilt became illegal under the Dress Act of 1746, a law designed to subdue the Highland clans. Sir Walter Scott is often credited with rehabilitating the kilt as a national symbol. Nowadays, there are around 14,000 tartans, and kilts are widely worn by men for special occasions, particularly at weddings, graduations and rugby matches.

Along with whisky, shortbread, thistle and the stag, the tartan kilt is one of Scotland's most recognised symbols.

Loch Ness Monster

Seen from its shore, Loch Ness is
big, but, some might say, chilly and
uninviting. Miles and miles and miles
of nothing much. That emptiness may,
paradoxically, be what prompts the sense
of a mysterious presence in those dark
depths. And Loch Ness *is* deep:
up to 227m (745ft). Plenty of space for
who knows what to lurk. Hoaxes have
abounded; fantasy flourished; scientific
searches have been at best inconclusive,
but belief in the Loch Ness Monster still
persists. A Jurassic survival; a stranded
seal; a trick of the light or a tall story:
our Nessie is very definitely here to stay.

*If Nessie didn't exist, we'd have had to invent her
to keep ourselves and our visitors guessing.*

Castles

Scotland's first castles were defensive structures on top of hills with clear views to the surrounding countryside. When peace came to Scotland, the aristocracy wanted to live in better accommodation closer to amenities, so they built palaces and stately homes that combined luxury and sophistication with the outward visual appeal of the earlier structures. You can visit Edinburgh and Stirling castles, both examples of royal homes within earlier fortified structures, as well as great family homes that were built for peaceable times, such as Culzean Castle on the west coast and Lennoxlove House near the east coast.

Dunnottar Castle, near Stonehaven. Historic Scotland estimates that the nation has around 1,000 castles.

Rosslyn Chapel

So remarkable is medieval Rosslyn Chapel,
so strange, so eerie in its atmosphere that it's
almost a surprise to find that Dan Brown
didn't invent it. Its 15th-century stone carvings
are extraordinary in their pagan symbolism,
including a great many 'green men' (foliage-
clad faces, emblems of fertility) and what appear
to be corncobs, carved when corn (maize) was
still unknown in Europe. There may be older,
grander churches, but, between the Knights
Templar, the Freemasons, the Holy Grail and all
the rest, there can't be many that have inspired
quite so much fascinated speculation.
In 2015 a panel of the Great Tapestry of
Scotland depicting Rosslyn was stolen.

*Mysterious motifs carved on 213 stone blocks above the
altar have been interpreted as an encoded musical score.*

'Old' and 'New' Edinburgh

The Old Town and the New Town of
Edinburgh, which offer contrasting lessons
in urban planning, are together listed as
a Unesco World Heritage Site. The Old
Town, on a medieval plan, is a mish-mash of
styles, heights and twisting closes. The New
Town, by comparison, offers consistent
architecture on a cool Georgian grid,
reflecting the values of the Enlightenment.
Between the two, on Calton Hill, is the
time ball, which is dropped at 1PM each day
to allow sailors on the Forth to adjust their
chronometers. The One o' Clock gun, fired
daily from Edinburgh Castle since 1861, is a
fog-proof backup.

*The original geometric street plan for the New Town
has undergone several stages of alteration and addition.*

Scotland's Great Architects

Charles Rennie Mackintosh, who thought of himself as much an artist as an architect, brought all of his talents to bear on the magnificent Glasgow School of Art (built 1899–1909, damaged by fire in 2014). Margaret Macdonald, Mackintosh's wife, deserves credit for many of Mackintosh's interiors. Scotland's other world-class architects include Robert Adam (Charlotte Square in Edinburgh, Culzean Castle in Ayrshire), Alexander 'Greek' Thomson (St Vincent Street Church, Glasgow), Robert Lorimer (Scottish National War Memorial in Edinburgh Castle) and J J Burnet (Cenotaph in Glasgow and various First World War memorials in Europe).

The Glasgow School of Art, an early modern masterpiece, is one of the most important Scottish buildings of the 20th century.

Clydeside Shipbuilding

Glasgow made the Clyde, goes the
saying, and the Clyde made Glasgow.
By deepening and straightening the
river, the city opened up a direct route
to the Atlantic, and became the only
Victorian city that was both a port and
a manufacturing centre. Early maritime
traders included the 18th-century Tobacco
Lords, who made fortunes from importing
tobacco from Virginia. Shipbuilders
launched ships of all sizes, from transatlantic
liners to the humble Clyde Puffer, which
was a familiar sight all over the western
seaboard. The history of the Clyde and its
ships can be seen in the Riverside Museum.

*From 1909 to 1913 Clyde shipbuilders launched
more than a fifth of world maritime tonnage.*

Weaving and Textiles

Scotland's worldwide reputation for excellence in textiles is second to none. Harris Tweed has been handmade for centuries, from the pure wool of hardy Hebridean sheep, dyed with lichen, hand spun, and woven in traditional patterns. Fair Isle knitwear, originating from a remote island lying between Orkney and Shetland, is equally coveted, with its distinctive horizontal geometric patterning formed by knitting with multiple colours. Dundee, the city of jute, jam and journalism, built its considerable Victorian wealth on processing jute from India, while other parts of Scotland specialised in cotton, linen, lace and silk.

Around 50,000 workers toiled in 60 jute mills in Dundee. Their story is told at the restored 19th-century Verdant Works.

Stitches in Time

Bayeux might have its tapestry, but it's dwarfed by the Great Tapestry of Scotland, which is 143m (469ft) long. The brainchild of author Alexander McCall Smith, and designed by Andrew Crummy, the Tapestry tells Scotland's story from pre-history to modern times. Each of the 160 embroidered panels depicts an episode from Scotland's history, and the whole thing required 65,000 hours of stitching and 480km (300 miles) of wool, making it one of the biggest ever community arts projects in Scotland. The Tapestry has toured venues all over the country and been exhibited at the Scottish Parliament.

The tapestry depicts everything from the Ice Age to the recreation of the Scottish Parliament in 1999.

Classic Scottish Writers

Robert Burns, James Hogg and Sir Walter
Scott stride over the early 19th century,
with stories and poems firmly rooted in the
folklore and people of Scotland. Robert
Louis Stevenson (*Treasure Island, Kidnapped,
Jekyll and Hyde*) and Sir Arthur Conan
Doyle (*Sherlock Holmes* stories, *The Lost
World, The White Company*) commanded
the second half of the century and the
beginning of the next with larger-than-life
characters and page-turning plots that are
still inspiring filmmakers and other writers.
Burns Night is celebrated worldwide every
January, and Doyle's greatest character is
regularly given a modern makeover.

*Long John Silver, the pirate villain of Treasure Island,
is one of Scotland's most famous fictional characters.*

Modern Scottish Literature

Scotland inspired many writers in the 20th century, not least J K Rowling, creator of a certain boy wizard. George Heriot's School, visible from her favourite writing spot in central Edinburgh, was the inspiration for Hogwarts. Earlier in the century, Hugh MacDiarmid and Edwin Muir in poetry and Lewis Grassic Gibbon and John Buchan in the novel presented a wider range of Scottish experience than Scott or Stevenson had. The Broons, Oor Wullie and Desperate Dan entertained young readers. Current stars include Alexander McCall Smith, Kate Atkinson, Michel Faber and Ian Rankin. A new wave of crime writers gave rise to the expression 'Tartan Noir'.

Schooling (and perhaps a little sorcery?) helped Edinburgh become the first UNESCO City of Literature in 2004.

Highland Games

Scots have enjoyed sports such as tossing the caber, wrestling, the tug of war and throwing the hammer since time immemorial, but the Highland Games we know and love today is mainly a Victorian invention. Along with the athletic events, a typical Games features dancing, piping and drumming competitions, and a general celebration of all things Scottish. The Cowal Games, held in Dunoon, is Scotland's largest, attracting some 3,000 competitors and more than 20,000 spectators every year. But Highland Games are now also popular around the world, with events held everywhere from Brazil to Indonesia, from New Zealand to the USA.

In caber tossing, it's not how far the caber is tossed that's important, but how straight it falls.

The Home of Golf

The course at St Andrews claims to be 'Royal and Ancient', but its foundation in 1754 makes it something of a parvenu: golf was played at Edinburgh's Bruntsfield and Leith Links (and very likely elsewhere) long before. Exactly where this venerable sport teed off remains uncertain, but there's no serious question that it started here in Scotland. No wonder, then, that this country attracts players from all over the world to pit their skills against the famous courses, from Gullane to Gleneagles, from Turnberry to Troon and Trumpton – and often in conditions windy enough to blow a toupé clean off the head.

Scotland has more golf courses per head than any other country. Oh, and did we mention they are the world's best?

Sporting Scotland

There's more to Scottish sport than golf, the Old Firm and Highland Games. For a start there's tennis ace and Wimbledon champion Andy Murray, from Dunblane. Sir Chris Hoy has won an astonishing six Olympic gold medals and is such a successful cyclist that they even named Glasgow's state-of-the-art velodrome after him. Our curling teams are up there with the very best in the world, and Glasgow played host to the Commonwealth Games in 2014, with Scotland achieving its best-ever medal haul, coming fourth overall. Plus, don't forget the thousands of Scots who hike, bike, ski, kayak, sail or swim in a country seemingly purpose-built for outdoor sports.

The CairnGorm Mountain Railway takes skiers and hikers (and wheelchair users) to enjoy the views over Strathspey.

Scottish Art and Artists

The Reverend Robert Walker, pictured skating on Duddingston Loch in the 1790s, was immortalised in oils by Edinburgh's Henry Raeburn – one of a long line of artists to depict Scotland's people, landscapes and conceptual themes and putting a distinctive Scottish art on the international map. The Glasgow Boys (such as A E Hornel), the Scottish Colourists (including J D Fergusson) and the sculptor Eduardo Paolozzi have all created distinctively Scottish art of international significance. The Glasgow School of Art has an extraordinary record of producing Turner Prize nominees and winners; reflecting this, the city hosted the 2015 Turner Prize – its first time in Scotland.

Henry Raeburn's 'Skating Minister' is one of the most iconic paintings in Scottish art.

Artists at the Seaside

The fishing village of Kirkcudbright on the Solway coast may be one of Britain's least pronounceable places outside Wales (it's 'Ker-Coo-Bree'), but it is a delightful place: a lively, bustling community, with a ruined castle, harbour and neatly laid-out streets. Above all, the town is picturesque – literally: an artist's colony formed here in the 1880s. The Glasgow Boys and Scottish Colourists painted its buildings, boats and beautiful surrounds, as do budding artists today. With its stunning shores and views, the isle of Iona was another magnet for the Colourists – notably, F C B Cadell. Scenic Plockton in the Highlands is another artists' favourite.

Kirkcudbright's sheltered harbour has been in use for millennia, as evidenced by nearby stone circles, forts and Roman ruins.

Kelvingrove

This is the Glasgow that many outsiders know little of: leafy, peaceful, even genteel. And cultured, with a capital 'C': in its beautiful parkland setting by the River Kelvin, the Kelvingrove Art Gallery and Museum attracts connoisseurs from around the world to see its dinosaurs and Dalí. The University of Glasgow has been here since the 15th century, plenty of time for the student atmosphere to become established. Glasgow's *Rive Gauche*, the West End is full of high-toned life, with lots of cafés, restaurants and quirky shops. It's a great place simply to stroll and enjoy the atmosphere.

This entrance to the museum was, according to an urban myth, intended to face the park at the rear of the building.

Statues and Public Art

The largest equine sculpture in the world, the
30-metre-high Kelpies were created by the
sculptor Andy Scott, already known for his
Heavy Horse alongside the M8 motorway,
and other installations. The steel-built Kelpies
opened to the public in April 2014 at The
Helix, by the Forth & Clyde Canal near Falkirk.
They represent a mythical water animal with
mighty strength, and weigh in at 300 tonnes
each. Scotland boasts many monuments, from
prehistoric standing stones to contemporary art.
The most famous statue today may be the one
of Wellington in Glasgow's Royal Exchange
Square: it's almost always seen with a traffic
cone upon the equestrian's head.

*Stags and Highland coos may be more frequently spotted in
Scotland than horses, but equines dominate the public art world.*

Edinburgh's Festivals

'The world's leading festival city,' says the marketing spiel, and it's hard to disagree. Science, storytelling, film and the visual arts all have their own festivals in Edinburgh, and it's the summer when the festival season really takes over the city. The whole place comes alive during the International Festival with thrilling music, dance, theatre and opera, whilst the Festival Fringe sees comedians and budding artists perform literally hundreds of alternative shows every day. At the same time there's the Royal Edinburgh Military Tattoo, and great writers appear at the Book Festival. But perhaps the biggest party comes in winter with the Hogmanay celebrations.

The fireworks display has become a hugely popular part of the grand finale of the International Festival.

Inventions and Innovations

James Watt, a Scottish engineer and entrepreneur, perfected the steam engine, which replaced water power as the driving force of industry. Other Scottish innovators include Lord Kelvin (transatlantic cable, absolute zero), Alexander Graham Bell (telephone), John Logie Baird (television), and more recently Ian Donald (medical ultrasound), Ian Wilmut and colleagues (Dolly the Sheep, the first mammal cloned from an adult cell), Nobel Prize-winner Peter Higgs, and a raft of computer-game creators. Many examples of Scottish ingenuity, including a stuffed Dolly, are on display in the National Museum of Scotland in central Edinburgh.

Dolly the Sheep was named after Dolly Parton. Backing singers were a missed opportunity, perhaps.

Frae Haggis tae Cakes

Traditionally made from 'sheep's pluck' (heart, liver and lungs), onion, oatmeal, suet, spices and salt, haggis is not for the faint-hearted. But one mouthful will help you understand why Rabbie Burns declared it the 'chieftain o' the pudding race'. Aberdeen Angus is considered the finest beef, with Scottish salmon and many varieties of shellfish being in demand well beyond our shores. But we're also a 'land o' cakes': Tunnocks teacakes even featured in the opening ceremony of Glasgow's 2014 Commonwealth Games. The Dundee cake was reportedly the favourite of Mary, Queen of Scots; she's also credited with inventing shortbread, now a veritable symbol of Scotland.

Haggis, neeps and tatties form the heart of a Burns Supper. Salmon, Dundee cake and Tunnocks are all braw, too.

Whisky Galore

Taking its name from the Gaelic *uisge beatha* ('water of life'), whisky is a big earner for the economy and central to our identity – it's truly the spirit of Scotland. Distilling grain mash to produce a strong alcoholic drink has taken place for centuries, but it only made the leap into sophisticated tipple during the 18th century. Now, 'Scotch' whisky is a byword for quality around the world, and there's also recently been a huge increase in artisan breweries creating top real ales. And if you indulge too much? There's always 'Scotland's other national drink', Irn-Bru, popularly regarded as a hangover cure.

Scotland's distilleries are grouped in five regions: Highland, Speyside, Lowland, Islay and Campbeltown.

Polyglot Nation

English is the standard language of
Scotland, spoken in a variety of dialects
(from cut-glass Morningside in Edinburgh
to rough-and-tough Glaswegian). Scots,
also called Lallans, is the historical native
version of English, and the Celtic language
Gaelic (pronounced gaa-lick) is strongest
in the north and west Highlands and
Islands. Thanks to multiculturalism,
visitors to the cities are likely to encounter
Polish, Romanian or Russian from eastern
Europe or Urdu, Punjabi or Chinese from
eastern Asia. Most people understand
American and Canadian, but struggle with
French and German.

*About 60,000 people in Scotland speak Gaelic. The rest are
convinced that the spelling is designed to confuse outsiders!*

FAE SCHOLARS

Glossary

auld – old

ben – a mountain peak

bonnie – attractive or beautiful

brae – a bank, slope or hillside

Braveheart – Mel Gibson movie about William Wallace

braw – good

Burns Night – annual celebration of Robert Burns' birthday, 25 January

Caledonia – Roman/Latin name for Scotland

ceilidh – a traditional Gaelic social event

Celts – historical peoples in Scotland, Wales and Ireland (and once across Europe)

Central Belt – the densely populated 'waistline' of Scotland, including Ayrshire, Edinburgh, Falkirk, Fife, Glasgow and the Lothians

coo – cow

Corbett – a Scottish mountain over 2,500ft (762m)

crannog – an artificial 'island', often simply a house or a basic fortified building on stilts

croft – a small rented farm where land is held in common with neighbouring farms

dreich – dreary, bleak, miserable weather

dun – Gaelic word for 'fort'

firth – an estuary or sea inlet

frae – from

Gaelic – a Celtic language

glen – valley

Hielan' – Highland

Highlands – historical north-east region of Scotland, dominated by mountain ranges

ilka – each or every

Jacobite – a supporter of the Catholic King James Stuart (and his heirs) and their claim to the throne. The name derives from Jacobus, the Latin form of James

loch – a lake or narrow sea inlet

Lowlands – historical region of Scotland lying to the south and east of the Highlands

machair – low-lying coastal grassland made up of sand and shell fragments blown ashore by the Atlantic winds

midgie – tiny flying insects that bite

Munro – a Scottish mountain over 3,000ft (914m)

neeps – a dish of mashed turnips (although, confusingly, the English call them 'swedes'!)

Nessie – the Loch Ness Monster

Old Firm – the collective name for Celtic and Rangers, Glasgow's two major football clubs

Picts – early medieval peoples of northern and eastern Scotland

raised beach – former beach now lying above water level

'Scotch Mist' – a heavy, wet mist that's almost drizzly rain

sea stack – a vertical column of rock standing in the sea

'Skating Minister' – Henry Raeburn painting of Reverend Robert Walker

Soay – breed of sheep originally from St Kilda

tae – to

tatties – potatoes (mashed, in a traditional Burns Supper)

Trainspotting – a cult book by Irvine Welsh about drug addicts in Edinburgh. Later made into a film by Danny Boyle and starring Ewan McGregor

wee – small

Weegie – a Glaswegian

wha' – who

Whisky Galore! – a book and film about a real-life shipwreck bestowing a cargo of whisky on Scottish islanders

wynd – a narrow lane or alleyway between buildings

Index

Jumped Up Publishing
Bookspeed
16 Salamander Yards
Edinburgh, EH6 7DD

Artwork by Adam Larkum, ink-tank + associates

Created and produced by Saraband, Glasgow, for JUP

Written by Michael Kerrigan and Ronnie Scott (for the
history chapter), with Craig Hillsley and Sophie Franklin.
Editor: Sara Hunt

ISBN: 9780955364150

Printed in the EU on sustainably sourced paper.

1 2 3 4 5 6 7 8 9 10